MW00586278

Greater Is He

A Child Abuse Survivor's Collection of Poems

Kerry Kinlaw

Copyright © 2020, Kerry Kinlaw

Printed in the United States of America
Third Edition

First Printing, 2019

ISBN: 978-1-7349460-9-3

Kinlaw Books

Therapeutic Literature

Little Rock, Arkansas

Dedication

This book is dedicated to all those who suffer in silence. To those who are still trying to piece together their shattered lives because of abuse suffered at the hands of a parent.

You are not alone. There is hope and healing available to you. Don't suffer in silence. Speak about the things that bother you. Forgive those who caused you pain. Releasing the pain provides freedom to you and allows you to live a life full of peace.

I know because I survived.

A Tribute

The image for the book cover was chosen in homage to my Aunt Dolores. Aunt Dolores played a very pivotal role in my life as a child. I wouldn't have recovered as well as I did if she hadn't interceded in my life.

Aunt Dolores loves elephants.

Thank you, Aunt Dolores, for giving me a mother's love when I needed it most.

Table of Contents

"Ye are of God, little children,
and have overcome them:
because greater is he that is in you,
than he that is in the world."
1 John 4:4 (KJKV)

Foreword

Meeting Mr. Kinlaw was kismet.

I believe that in the earth there are echoes that reverberate in our lives. These echoes happen when God is adamant about getting His point across.

God's word will not return void. So, when He says it, it is so!

First, I wrote a book about my childhood trauma and how secrets and shame held me captive.

Then, on a call an author spoke about how we not only have to acknowledge our issues, but we have to confront them.

The very next day, I spoke with Mr. Kinlaw and while telling me about his book, he informed me that in essence it had taken him more than 30 years to understand that childhood trauma doesn't disappear no matter how badly we may want it to.

One thing I learned as I wrote my memoir is that the saying, "What happens in your home, stays in your home" is a tragic lie. The things that happen to us follow us and if we refuse to acknowledge them and confront them, they not only remain, they grow.

Kudos to Mr. Kinlaw for acknowledging his truth and sharing his story so that others may heal.

Iris M. Williams/*An Abundant Life: The Trilogy*

for every kid who has a story to tell...

Acknowledgments

To my sisters and brother – I love you.
We still stand.
We are still here.
We survived and I'm thankful God allowed me
to share my story to free others
from their bondage of pain.
**Chiniqua, Keeshanona "Kissa", Robert,
Louvenia & Malika**

Prologue

If my English teacher had told me I would pen a book, I would have laughed. I was the class clown. Perhaps this was because I grew up in a home without much to laugh about. I wasn't popular, but most people knew me. Evidence of that is the fact that I am on the front page of my graduating class high school's yearbook giving love to the Principal.

Like physical wounds, emotional wounds do not magically disappear. As a matter of fact, *that* is the prologue of *Greater Is He*. The word prologue is multifaceted and can be defined in many ways. For the sake of brevity and clarity, I choose to use the definition found by google:

an event or action that leads to another event or situation

My war began when I was a child. Like many wars, not declared by the Commander in Chief, I didn't initiate it. I simply suffered from it. The effects of war are long, often lasting many years after the enemies' troops re-deploy back to their garrison. The same was true for me. The impact of my childhood trauma followed me into my adulthood, far past my interaction with the enemy.

Outwardly (unless you've been physically injured), no one can even tell you if you have been to war or not. However, as a soldier, I understand more than most that you cannot measure the impact of war wounds.

I was fine. Or so I thought.

I graduated from high school. I attained the rank of a Senior Noncommissioned Officer in the United States Army. I married. I became a father. I was considered successful. However, it wasn't long before patterns began to emerge.

I realized I wasn't fine.

While I wanted to blame everyone, I couldn't escape the fact that the common denominator of my *sitz en leben* was not everyone else; it was me. I had to face the real possibility that the problem was me.

I was under the impression that I'd put my childhood trauma behind me. My teachers, mentors, friends, and counselors praised me for beating the odds. However, none of them told me that to *truly* overcome my past, I had to first face the things that happened to me as a kid.

Yes, I attained successful milestones according to societal standards, but when you experience childhood trauma at the hands of parents who had not overcome their own demons, the likelihood of continued success can be significantly compromised.

So, while reaching those milestones was important, it paled in comparison to the task of maintaining them.

In my family, there were six of us, and each of us was affected differently. While not all survivors of childhood abuse are impacted the same, one thing psychology supports is that there is indeed impact, and it needs to be addressed.

My story may not be your story. Maybe your trauma didn't hinder you. Mine did.

Greater Is He, is my awakening, the precursor to my journey.

Many of these poems are the beginning embers of the roaring wildfires burning in the backdrops of my life. On the pages that follow, I attempted to capture the good, the bad, and the ugly.

Life is messy and multifaceted. Healing and strength don't happen magically. It is the by-product of arduous tough introspection, calling a spade a spade, seeking therapy, and gaining insight.

I found out that I am not an anomaly. Children who go through the things I have, sometimes struggle. That realization normalized the process. I had struggled silently and alone because I thought I was messed up. I thought I was broken. I thought I was alone. I was an abused child. I needed to reconcile that abuse with my adult mind.

Review the table of contents, and when a title jumps out at you, read it. Do not allow the ugliness to hinder you from witnessing the beautiful process of the transformation.

I am not my abuse, and neither are you.

Face your demons. Reconcile your past for the betterment of your life and the lives of generations to come.

Grab a seat, curl up with a good pillow, and find strength and courage as I tell you my story.

Best wishes on your journey,

MaskedPoet

You are not the Same

(A Marine Master Sergeant was leaving Stonington a
co-occurring rehab facility. He had "done the work" as
with most rehabs they take away or separate you
from the real reason you were drinking, abusing drugs
or alcohol. I could feel his apprehension I do not
remember ever having a knack for poetry but once I
read this to him and the group, I felt inspired to write)

When you first got here you were nervous anxious
and overwhelmed
You lacked fear and Godfidence
Life had put you through the wringer
You had enough
Yet there was another hit and enough for one more
drink
Your wife and career on the brink
Your mind was in a fog; if you could only think
So, here's your doctor and clinician
Promising to be the help for someone in our
condition
Let's talk; let's get deep
Maybe one day we can make you weep
Don't be afraid to cry; let's unearth Satan's lie
Time went fast time was fun
Now you're almost done
Where do you go from here?
You're still a user, so you wonder
Scared and afraid to make the next blunder
But you got this

You're not the same
You're almost free from life's pain
Your mind is clear
You're no longer insane
You're alive you're free
Yes, things are looking up
But are you free from the cup?
Time will tell
Your heart is starting to swell
You've talked it out its starting to make sense
Don't worry about tomorrow this is for today
Get it done make it count
Not one sip not one ounce
You are not the same.

WHAT'S IN THE BOX

So, I walked into my

life's garage

similar to a mirage

there is a shelf along

the wall

like in a bathroom

stall

full of boxes short

and tall

I've seen them before

going through them

will be a chore

the sadness felt to

the core

going through them is

the only way

to even the score

not even sure I want

to know

what they store

I stood paralyzed and

I felt the terror rise

I needed to

strategize

to ensure I wouldn't

be hypnotized

my doctor thought it

best

to slowly and carefully

address

as I decide what to do

next

a little perplexed so I

bent down to inspect

didn't know what to

expect

Greater is He

moved things around

to check

a photo album piqued

my interest

a brief moment of

distress

so, I grabbed the

album and I opened it

up pages upon pages

but what's on the

front

the only thing my mind

wants

is coming in and out of

focus

wonder what it

exposes

this journey isn't a

bed of roses

so, I come back to

myself I need some

help

who could assist it's

hard not to resist?

or to put it back in

the box

heart heavy as rocks

I need a spot

beam me up Scotty

as suggested

I selected two others

to spot me

back to my movie had

me feeling woozy

but these two had me;

had my back

so, I refused to

backtrack

Greater is He

took all the

confidence I had

I was really glad

my sister and Andrea

made me feel safe

standing with me in

that space

they could see the

worry on my face

they didn't chasten or

hasten

standing as I was

facing

my heart was racing

standing still but felt

like I was pacing

so, I calmed down

and I tried to enjoy

the moment

even though I was

spent

I relished the courage

it took

to reach in and grab

the photo book

MY SECRETS KEEP ME SAFE

I'll reveal them at my pace

keep them deep buried within

I'm afraid; been to war so they call me brave

I won't I can't share em'

I can't I won't bare em'

they're mine they're mine I'll say

if I free them my soul will fray

I'm frightened as I reveal

my chest will tighten

the fear will surely heighten

"Share them; share them

my load will lighten!"

"Tell the truth!"

"Be sure to be honest!"

"It is freeing!" is my doctor's promise

I'm paralyzed, my ankles are in a fetter.

So, I shared them and felt a little better.

I want to move, my face ashamed

my blood flees, as I portioned the pain

tears refuse to flow, like the winters refusal to

snow.

my secrets keep me safe

I keep them in my secret place

I won't, I can't reveal!

I can't, I won't unpeel!

you pull, you prod keeping me safe is my secret's

job.

or so I think

as my soul begins to sink

the weight is overbearing!

crying is for the sharing!

just let them go!

bit by bit blow by blow

take my time and I'll go slow

give myself a chance

release my mantra

say a chant

I can't stop now

I don't know how

I should tell unlock the keys to my cell

I want to be free

show and tell the real me

I'm out I'm out

if all goes well, I'll be free from my hell

It's getting deep

It's getting hot

I'm taking a chance

I'll take the shot

It's starting to feel really good

standing were others stood

sharing my pain

releasing the saga

some pain and some trauma

telling others about my momma

she was A BEAST

she was MY MONSTER

she kept me down

she made me frown

I couldn't laugh

I couldn't smile

unknowing the pain would last a while

38 and I'm still mad

mourning the childhood, I never had

SUFFERED in silence

so much violence

bruises covered by my clothes

hear my sadness hear my woes

walking on my tiptoes

afraid to stand

I don't feel like much of a man

nothing to offer

selling my worth to Satan's proffer

O and I'm guilty too I've made myself blue

pangs of sadness

selling my soul for another's gladness

you want me to dance

you want me to shuck

I want to be free

free to be unstuck

free from anger

free to care

free to give a fuck

I'll end it here

thanks for lending me your ear

so much is hidden I have another agenda

to free my mind

to loosen the bands

as I drop the mic from my hands

MY TRAUMA

As I desired to catalog my

       saga

anguish comes to mind

at the thought of my trauma

searching deep within

trying to capture my
emotions with this pen
I tried hard as hell to
describe my cell
darkness fills the room fear
surely looms
a picture of my mother who
traumatized me
my sisters and brother
Did she love us?
Couldn't I have been born to
another?
she caused such pain and so
much sorrow
it's no wonder I am so hollow
so empty
so dead
no words to shed
what words to use to
transcribe my abuse

I search
deeper and deeper, I want
the emotions
to bring them into focus
to put them into perspective
the words feel so elusive
it'll come one day
or is that just something
people say
I'm still on the surface
I feel the rumblings before
quake
this isn't my stop I say to
the conductor
speaking softly to the
trucker
I've got miles to share and
stories to bare
my stories are long
like notes to songs

full of pain and full of drama

my sadness comes from my

momma

she was fierce she was

tough

she made my childhood

rough

tears start to roll

as I ponder my hearts

treasure trove

filled to the brim with

sadness

so, I drink away the madness

traveling through life

attempting to avoid the

strife

you can cut the tension with

a knife

looking for a soft place to

land

without a pot

without a plan

looking through my window

where does the pain go?

how deep how far down it

takes a toll

I'm starting to drown

I need to bare this soul

but I don't want to tell a

soul of the pain

I carry

or the pain I endured

physical emotional injure

my mom's the culprit

lock her away refusing my

laughter

and thoughts of play

I must rise from these

ashes

give my sermon to the
masses
I long to share because I
long to heal
I long to reveal more
to share of the grief, I bare
please don't stare
I must find a way
there are things I must say
I refuse to sway
the nights are long no one
else
can sing my song the lashes
made me strong
I didn't break I wouldn't
bend
waiting for this pain to end
no relief in sight
not a soul to bear this plight
I feel alone just her tone

I knew I was in the wrong
when my name was called
in a song Kerry Levonne
laid across a kitchen chair
I wouldn't run I wouldn't
dare
still, I stayed even when the
lashes were laid
all sins must be paid
I wasn't tough I wasn't
brave
her anger I had to stave
why was she so angry?
Did I do wrong? crossed my
mind all along
queue the badness queue the
sadness
not much gladness but we
had each other me
my sisters and brother

I could go on because I
hated the summer no
reprieve from my mother
when school was out, we
hungered
we sat in darkness when it
thundered
when it rained, it poured
same sheet different chord
punished with chores
my childhood wasn't like
yours
wiping walls scrubbing floors
and all the dishes in the
cupboards
to name a few
the rent was due
woken in the middle of the
night

for a chore not done right
DYFS was called but didn't
help
too many children not
enough shelf
three foster homes
no place to call my own
couldn't wait till I was grown
then whatever I suffered
would be my own
that's what you think like a
cog in a kink,
not a blink
cuz you gotta deal
you gotta be real
deal with your stuff
no matter how rough

LETTER TO MY MOMMA

Because I didn't tell you
how I felt
my importance was put
on the shelf
in all honesty, I felt
what I felt
I have to own them for
my health
they weren't wrong and
they were true
bear with me because
this is new
I hated it when you beat
me with your shoe
the extension cord and
two by four too
I was sad most thought
I was bad
but anger was all I had
it wasn't a phase or a
fad

you could have been
nicer just a tad
so much abuse I was
just a lad
I felt ashamed full of
blame
maybe disdained
unexplained a little lame
maybe never the same
I thought I was insane
maybe to blame
YOU, I couldn't tame
overwhelmed and
overpowered
"Was I a coward?"
as I cower in a corner
thought I was a goner
destined to be a loner
because I couldn't
dethrone her
short not much a tower
but you had so much
power

couldn't imagine the
trouble I was in
thought being strong
meant to
take it on the chin
thought I had to bear it
learning how to share it
takes a tremendous
amount of grit
onest on you it sits,
blame, quite a bit
thought I was over it
but truly hadn't dealt
afraid to see you with a
belt
or anything else
doing this for self
again, this is for my
health

so, I don't swindle my
wealth
my peace of mind
"Were you blind?"
how come you couldn't
see
how much you affected
me
I JUST WANT TO BE
FREE
own your responsibility
take your part
while I refresh my heart
a nice restart, another
chance to start
forgiven for your part
and that's a start

TOUGH BEGINNING

I remember the white house

on South Pearl Street

the place where I was beat

the place I was scared to eat

the place where I suffered

tremendous defeat

where I was told to have several seats

the place I gave away my peace

I was a child living in the wild

subjected to my mom's parenting style

where most of my trauma is piled

my soul was reviled

I'm stronger now

it's a process how

I refused to let this trauma

cause another moment of dishonor

I just gotta, keep getting up

with any luck

I will no longer be stuck

as my colleges say embrace the suck

to give a fuck

to raise a muck

to declare it was yuck

refuse to duck

my past is the past

it won't always last

unfortunately, it's not fast

but that was my beginning

it was tough

LIFE STORY

July 27, 1980 Melody my mother had me,
she was 19

let me paint the scene

already had another sister

maybe by the same mister

back to me and my twin sister

premature, small and red

Virginia born, Jersey bred

the three of us grew up in the same bed

my nanny was still around

shortly she was laid in the ground

cancer is what they found

mind blown, couldn't believe she was gone

she saved us a few times

when mom didn't spare the pine

grabbed a switch naked and without a stitch

my mom found Rick

when she played an ugly trick

he was a wreck when he found

she had stolen his check

a fight ensued he became unglued

mom was cut

she never told him where the check was put

we awoke early in the day

didn't even put the dishes away

on the road and we were gone

no notice none

we thought it was just for fun

but now I feel like we were on the run

it's four of us now

all in the back and I don't know how

yes, mom had another my younger brother

headed to New Jersey, stopped at the home of a park called Hershey

didn't see a lark until we parked

drove until dark we pulled up to a nice house, clean as can be with no mouse

you could tell we were from the south

the accent of our mouth was a good clue

meeting an aunt we never knew

sweet lady named Aunt Dolores with a dog as big as a horse Great Dane mixed with German Sheppard

with a cat as fat as a Leopard

this was family

she made us as comfortable as can be

offered us a dish with candy

married to an uncle who was handy

we stayed here for a while

she didn't like moms parenting style

they went at it until mom had had it

mom was mean, kept us lean

all nightmares not a sweet dream

never any ice-cream or any dessert

she kept us hurt missed a few growth spurts

we were tiny little squirts short for our ages

mom sabotaged our beginning stages

read books by the pages

started school learned the rules

my aunt still cramping my mom's style

moved away, about a mile

maybe two, the house was new

the carpet was blue, ate on them too

laid out newspaper a few layers

until we got a table

didn't get to watch cable

I don't know if my mom was stable

no TV, we weren't able

neglected and abused

didn't think anyone had a clue

my cousin gave my mom a hard time too

mom beat us until we were black and blue

all alone now mom is on the throne

no love to make this house a home

so I drop lyrics to this poem

mom was putting us through the wringer

no canary, but now I'm a singer

told DYFS (division youth and family services)
about our saga, teachers spied the drama

don't get me wrong I loved my momma

but she was the cause of the trauma

neglected and ordered upstairs

life wasn't fair

greeted with a mean mom stare

wondered did she care

whoopings she didn't spare

talk back I didn't dare

needed a fresh breath of air

laid across a chair

no love was shared there

locked in a basement

like solitary confinement

moments spent in the dark

longed to be a lark, so I could be free

kids didn't envy me

had to ask to pee

kicked out of my home, forced to roam

home after home, on my own felt alone

three foster homes, not much shalom

moved to Alvin's he was kin my great uncle

still I was in trouble

more trauma on the double

I was angry and confused

because I was abused

acted a fool in school

kids thought I was cool

mainly misunderstood

my uncle didn't spare the wood

beat me when he could

not for nothing, always for something

I couldn't trust then

always abandoned was the sentence

handed back to my momma's

act three of my trauma

same momma

same drama

comma after comma

beatings in the middle of the night

for chores not done right

Was this my lot in life?

Was this my forever plight?

I couldn't fight something isn't right

I remember parts of the night

don't remember what she did

but momma blacked my sisters eyelid

the end of my prisons bid

now I was my aunts' kid

a kid again

that was the beginning to the end

of my trauma and my saga

I RAN OUT OF BOXES

I thought I was given a gift

because I didn't trip

when life flipped the script

I thought I was supernaturally strong

boy I was supernaturally wrong

I had all these boxes in my head

a box for every time

life made me want to cry

a box for every time I questioned why

a box for every lie

a box for when life wasn't sweet as pie

a box for every time I'd rather die

a box for every time it rained

for every time I was drained

as long as I had boxes I felt sly as the foxes

slicker than oil

a box was considered my spoil

trophies of bad memories

trophies of perceived victories

as long as I had boxes I never questioned my moxie

I was never a softy

took a licking and kept on ticking ticking

like a Timex

so I didn't expect

when I went to my shelf

and there were no boxes left

a shelf full of boxes

boxes stored away

that never saw the light of day

I always looked the other way

because I always took what may

but this is a new day

looked to the left looked to the right

not a box in sight

I am pretty sure I last seen them there

but there wasn't a box anywhere

now I'm nervous and in despair

"Does anyone have a box to spare?'

totally caught unaware

a box for every care

a box for every burden to bear

what do I do now

cuz I lost my how

I refuse to sweat

refuse to fret

my system hasn't failed me yet

let me regroup

Had I been duped?

Where were the boxes of everything scooped?

I was getting pooped, tired and starting to sweat

I was starting to fret

I made it all this time

even though life hadn't been kind

I'd never been in a bind

but I was starting to unwind

my gears came to a slow grind

they didn't stop

but may pops will eventually pop

the second shoe will find a way to drop

it wasn't easy but life wasn't breezy

it started to tease me

I fought as long as I could

longer than others thought I would

life brought me to my knees

no boxes for my pleas

so I admitted defeat that I had been beat

now life has become sweet

it's not a flip of a switch

or a scratch of an itch

even felt naked clothes with stitches

can anyone suture my past to my future unite them together

to make everything better

it taught me many lessons

my pain might be my biggest blessing

I no longer want to wrestle

I decided to be a vessel

a martyr of sorts a champion of sports

a powerful support my

message is clear

you must get over the fear

and deal with your issues

the pain you don't deal with will eventually lick you

I CRIED TODAY

tears rolled down
the sides of my face

They were
welcomed like a
sweet embrace

I cried today
because I didn't
come to play

I cried today
because my tears
have something to
say and I vowed to
never betray the
way I feel

I'm learning it is the
only way

to heal the right way
to deal

the best way to stay
even keel

so now I welcome
the pain

I choose to remove
the disdain

I'm not supercilious
but my previous
way didn't do me
much justice

So no more pushing
down the pain

I have my soul to
regain and a new
generation to train I
want my daughter
to know to take life
slow

life is a process

sometimes doesn't
do what's best

so sit back
sometimes you get
to steer

don't drown your
pain with beer
sometimes

you just have to
hold on

and feel each twinge

until the pain is
gone

but when pain
knocks at your door

even though it's a
chore take the heat

the graham crackers
allow the pain to
melt

the marshmallows
and make a smore

FEELINGS

For so long I couldn't name them

or claim them

they didn't serve so I gave them the swerve

silenced what I heard

need to be cured repressed or suppressed

both were for the best paved the way for my
success but that's in the past so to last

I've got to put them on blast

can no longer avoid them can no longer ignore
them expression is such a blessing

no regression - no repression - no suppression

in order to heal

I must address how I feel

THE JOURNEY

For some the climb
it's about getting to
the top

for some it's about
getting to the other
side

for me it's about
enjoying the ride

deliberately
intentionally willfully

looking at the trees
verse the forest life

isn't easy nor is it
easy to choose
what's best

so I reluctantly
address the hiccups
along the way bring
the falters to the
brightness of day

not discounting the
strays strays like
fuzz

strays from the way
sometimes life can
knock you off your
horse but I urge you
and me to enjoy the
course words like
mindful come to
mind don't rush it
the process takes
time you can wine
or ride the pine

but continue to
climb take a knee or
opportunity to rest
and catch a breath
and although we are
scared to death take
a step do another
rep talk to yourself
give yourself a pep
look deep introspect

be your best
cheerleader give
yourself a
motivational speech
repair the breech
and whatever you
do continue to reach
for some it's about

getting to the top
for some it's about
getting to the other
side for me it's
about enjoying the
ride

MOM COME HOLD ME

Momma come hold me console me

don't scold me the world is cold and lonely it's
a dark place without a warm embrace can't put
a name to the face

looked like I was sprayed with mace

no tears to taste such a waste

life came at such a fast pace

learning how to soothe myself

at an early age

skipped a stage

missed a page

but the war was waged

it's been hard to gage, hard to engage doomed
in my youth

before I had my first tooth

it's hard to face my truth

rather uncouth made me a sleuth

had to become a detective

my upbringing had me feeling defective later I
would become depressive not really knowing
what bothered me

couldn't remember it distinctively

the warzone I was raised in

had to embrace being thin

not set up for the win

full of questions like was this because of sin
need a doctor trained in spin

because it's hard to embrace my within

you weren't kind wish I could rewind

the hands of time

hated this life of mine

grew up without a spine

or an erector spinae

had to do things your way

I was grateful to see another day

I was scared to live and afraid to die

the conflict of my eye

the constant questions why

I'd rather hear a lie

than to know your reason why

I made it okay

in my head

I wanted to be dead

thought it would be fixed

when I was a newlywed

but I needed to be fed

I stayed in bed

I was up and moving

because I was picking and choosing

I was asleep at the wheel

couldn't name what I feel

couldn't face it either - bob and weave

quick to leave easy to deceive

hard to receive will it ever reprieve

will I ever breathe I need to grieve

and come to terms

possibly discern

the early lessons learned

EMPTY HANGERS

I remembered the
hangers today

they had clothes on
them

hanging this and
that way

maybe I'm berserk

when I left for work

a kiss on the
forehead off to work

we were supposed
to grab lunch

we had been in a
crunch

we argued we
cussed each other
out

there was plenty of
doubt

but I hoped we'd
work it out

let's talk about what
I believed

in certain
relationships, you
can't

just up and leave

trust me I get It

it was a cognitive
distortion

but believed denotes
past tense

bear with me for
traumas expense

there are some
relationships

you cannot grab
your ball and walk
away

you must stay and
play

through the
brightest and
darkest of days

illuminate the rays
whether sun or
moon

rainstorm or
monsoon

through thick
beginning of the
wick then

even wits beginning
to the end

see my mom had
already left

she didn't give a "f"

I guess no one had told her

Hell no one had told me

that when she did I would feel so empty

I would look all over the world

in the heart of every girl

under every unturned rock

through the tick-tock

from the hands of life's clock

Howard the duck stuck

embrace the suck

I mean I looked and looked

just like I looked for her letter

she didn't up and walk away she's better

I married her so she must be better

than mom

soiled my palms looking for your letter

Mom was grown

she didn't have to explain herself

she didn't leave it on the counter in a cabinet

or on the shelf

empty hangers to face myself

EMPTY HANGERS: PART TWO

The hangers aren't so bad

they represent a part of history just a tad

matter of fact

into focus out of abstract

I'm already too deep refuse to backtrack

if I gotta be honest

upfront direct lest

you'll miss the point

I did for all these years

maybe that's why I couldn't shed the tears

I've been mourning the loss

but hadn't removed the dross

it was tragic of course

my ex-wife wasn't the source

22 years before

I don't remember the hangers

but I know I packed

All my shirts and too few slacks

for the life of me,

I cannot remember whether it was March

or September

the sun was out the day I was sent away

it wasn't my volition or decision

mom says I kicked her during one of her

discipline sessions

if I go really slow take my time

travel through my mind

my brilliant resilient mind

who's protected me all this time

I have to let it know that I can handle the

sadness of that day

no child should be sent away

like a stray dog named bullet

I couldn't process lacked the skills needed

I had finally done the worse thing I could have

done, sitting in the sun

I was unlovable un-huggable

my malfunction had reached

the highest junction

when you make your mom turn her back

the love fund dipped into the black

I was to blame

Kerry was his name

couldn't be tame

all the acting out didn't bring about

the change I earnestly needed

I needed a mother's love

my daddy's hug

a gentle tug a little snug

this hole I dug wool pulled ellipses rug

too young to be smug

he was strong he had endured the abuse

and yet he still refused

he was afraid to be enthused

he was stubborn

and he's always been hard to break

for goodness sake

I couldn't break him

my soul and my inner 8-year-old

he has endured more than I ever could

more abuse than any soul should

he's very strong took sad songs

that makes everyone else blue

he hummed the notes too

he took the vicissitudes and made them into

beautiful artworks of wood

he took my rejection

used it as a powerful weapon

to cause this introspection

and brave this moment of reflection

misdirection

he took the empty hangers

and strung them into poems

for like strangers

so to all those that have been left without a
simple note on a shelf

it was their reflection of self

here's the letter you've been looking for

add more

hey, I left and I won't be back

addressed by me

selfishly me

SHE WOUNDED ME

Emphatically tragically ironically

she had wounds

and although I never saw the scars

or knew the cause

she was wounded

How do I know?

I have the scars to show

she stabbed me with her inability to love

selfishness can be a hell of a drug

In my DNA is a struggle to love myself

an inability and lack of desire

to prioritize my health

At the core of my essence, I bear the burden

of every occurrence of abuse

I long and look for

sought after the perfect excuse

she abused me surely

treated me poorly

emphatically tragically ironically

I can minimize make it small

choose not to acknowledge

what has befallen me

but it happened

it really happened

out of the land of make-believe

into the land of no reprieve

I have to reach into my deepest depths

pass the evidence of my scars to retrieve

the life I long to live

and the life I desire to give

she was wounded therefore

she wounded me

no one told me the pain

involved in this journey

knees would become weak and snapshots

would become blurry

it's humbling because I cannot be in a hurry

I have to arise early to get the worm the

healing I need and the healing I yearn

so as the doctor fully scrubs in

I prepare myself for the within

I look within it's an inside job

cannot snob

choose not to rob

there's a whole life

on the other side of this pain

I am no longer satisfied with the mundane

disdain or the blame game

mediocre small life with my might

I'll give it all I've got

I vow to fight

enlist others to battle

leaning up in the saddle

no longer willing to straddle

no vacillation or hesitation

I am worth it

I will birth it

I have big dreams and despite the fear

and what it seems

regardless of the messages I've survived

implicitly or implied

buried alive

my old man has died

now my therapists, clinicians, and my intuition

are my trained guides

SHE LEFT

I was out of breath cause she left

not one inkling

so I starting sinking

I've been left before what really is one more

there's nothing to explore

insomnia team no sleep not even a snore

heartbroken brokenness tore

deep sadness to the core

fore, really loud and large rain clouds

Cumulonimbus or Nimbostratus

all I know is rain

I pushed down the pain

as I was so oft trained

but the pain remained

it would show up at the darnedest times

when her leaving was the farthest from my

conscious mind

little did I know just cause I grew in age the

war was waged

and my soul refused to disengage until I

looked at the facts on the page

I couldn't act my wage

so one day I tore the page

out of my life's book

like a sneaky nimble crook

I stole a quick look

for years it was this huge monster

I never wanted to jostle

counted myself out

winning was plain impossible

carrying this pain to death plausible

so I wrapped it in a sack put it on my back

made it easy to carry

gave it to the wife I was going to marry

do something with this I said

I'm sick tired and fed up

the abrupt interruptions

I mean it was really rude

the biggest attitude

so I tied it up to stop the interruptions

put a pretty bow on it

in a pretty sack

yeah pain and trauma take that

you're not so bad

but why was I still sad

I was sad all the time

So, I grabbed my favorite wine

something to quiet my mind

but I wasn't blind

I couldn't hear it but I saw it

with her pretty sack and pretty bow

I could still smell her though

her bow didn't do anything for the scent

smelled her everywhere I went

consider myself a gent

gentleman gentle small giant

I had to untie it

Stonington told me I must look inside

I cried I tried I sighed hoped I died

cause I couldn't hide it anymore

it reached my core

my soul

I was out of control

no one knew

that's what I told myself

clearly dumb and deaf

a little blind too

what did the wine do

absolutely nothing

the pain was there when I awoke from my last
blackout

my near-death experience

high prices and clearance

it refused to bend

this is where me and my pain would end

I DON'T BLAME MY EX-WIFE

I don't blame my
ex-wife

seared my flesh with
a dull knife

but being married
to me was no bed of
roses

we had sweet days

cavities and tooth
decay

June 4th was a
rough one

there were many
sleepless nights

and long arguments

because I was hell-
bent

with a hellacious
temperament

I tried to love while
wounded

which resulted in a
bad experiment

love built on a faulty

premise and
hypothesis

lies told her and
myself...quoted I
got this...

I name the days the
pains

not to establish
blame

healing is my real
aim

so before you judge

and feel inclined to
nudge

my therapist says
because of the pain

in my past

control issues and
the desire

to have the last
word

yeah it posed more
like a need

but I had a greed
more than a need to
breathe

I had to avoid more
pain at all cost

I had to be the boss

the buck had to stop
with me

so now it stops
with me

I make all the   but it sure is lonely
decisions

GOODBYE

It's such a simple word it's expected and not
absurd don't just leave tell me bye I've been
left all my life cuts deeper than the sharpest
knife left by my wife because we had too much
strife left by my mom

no announcements no pom poms

I was sent to a car

didn't travel far

didn't cut the mustard didn't make the bar

no gold star I'm full of pain

someone decided to leave again

didn't bother to say why

I think sometimes I'd rather you lie

"Am I not worthy of a goodbye?"

wish I could cry

another painful blow to my inner 8-year-old

I wish I could hold him

people leave us on a whim

trying to be strong and take it on the chin

"Are we ever going to win?"

"Here we go again!"

another poem another pep talk

or we can just sit and sulk

but the truth is we aren't the hulk

this ish hurts opens wounds replaced messages

that were often rehearsed

"Are we cursed?"

"Are we doomed?"

must we always stay tuned and watch you
leave couldn't so much as to heave a deuce

I don't have any more juice

I also understand balance and prerogative

we have to let you live

and reject the pain you give

I'm not going to fib

ad lib adjust or make a fuss

young Kerry we are enough

just the two of us

we can't stop here we still gotta trust and
admit the pain and the sadness

own the madness

so tonight I'll try to hold you console you

for those that don't have a clue and refuse to
see others points of view we will not isolate
until dissipates or lengthen our gait we won't
run air quotes

until each twinge is gone

it is a full gone conclusion

even possible collusion

let's leave young Kerry see how much he can
take will he finally admit the heartbreak the
painful stake the soulful ache or will he grab

his mask and throw himself into the next task
or will he finally amass the strength to admit
and own his past

VICISSITUDES

vi·cis·si·tude

/vəˈsisəˌt(y)o͞od/

plural noun: vicissitudes

A change of circumstances or fortune, typically
one that is unwelcome or unpleasant.

The day you got
upset and told me I
couldn't see our
daughter until a
court order was
furnished

I'll say it again it
hurt two-fold

How do you become
so cold to someone
who wanted to grow
old with you?

give her an Oscar or
a Tony

blow me

I know it's harsh but
it hurts like hell
tears ducts start to
swell

got me feeling like
the biggest fool

so maybe it's three-
fold

tri fold napkin

yeah maybe I
should start blacking
out

I'm mad at myself
for playing the role
picked up what you
put down

brought and sold

yep I'm a clown

how could I fall so
deep when you
weren't mine to
keep

you had a girl so
why did I make you
my world

and although there's
more

what about my little
girl

she's too young to
understand that
daddy's doing what
he can

that you changed
the plan

you changed the
script now I no
longer have the
leading role but I
can't fold

I gotta roll

with the punches

depression by the
bunches

bananas and
Sunkist

how could you so
easily dismiss

pop or twist

off cap

remote zap

contributed to the
trap

laid in waste

such haste

bitter to taste

two years have
passed since the
accusal

that warranted my
removal

my upheaval

conspired evil

she was a pawn
played it well

pushed my soul
deeper into hell

skimming the
surface

lied about the
details

said or alluded that
I wanted more

honestly, it would've
been nice to score

body was banging
but the face was
hard on the
scorecard

I was honest cause
we spoke honestly

on a few occasions

under false
pretenses maybe
persuasion

this is purely
speculation

I imagine the others
launched a war used
you to even the
score

I was on track for
my E-8

on time not late

but you sealed my
fate

filled my plate

watched as the
opportunity
lengthened its gait

I must congratulate

you messed up my
world and dropped
the Mic

that kind of hurt led
me to psych

the phone call from
my commander

were the beginning
burning ambers

stuttering suffering
stammering

heart hammering

I believed my
history would plead
my case

15 years of positive
evaluations

17 plus years of
honorable service

to this nation

walked the hot
streets of Iraq

with a weapon and a
camel-back

trained the ICDC

sometimes alone in
the tower just me

completed missions

with my trigger
finger itching

faced fear that still
stalls me at night

did I say fight

long days cold
nights

cold gloved fingers
and frostbite

trips to MEPS

nights I wish I slept

moved every three
years

walked away from
friends I held dear

lost comrades cried
tears

missed moments
while on
deployments

nieces and nephews

passes and reviews

motor pool Mondays

in the field Sundays

stayed motivated
while agitated

bore military
bearing

stood still while my
leaders were
swearing

money wasted on
uniforms wearing

they call it the
military profession

it has its blessings

but wait while I
plead my case

the case should've
been dismissed
wasn't ready for the
plot twist

that list gave me
great confidence
that my profession
would have my back

took up the slack

racism cause I'm
black

but I was taken
aback

when I was told to
pack

on track to retire

talking about the
wire

now we talking
about fire

firing me

that list alone
couldn't condone

how could my love
quickly disown

I loved her and she
made me look good

had me figured out
thought she
understood

she turned me own
kept me on wood

promoted early
every time

based on
demonstrated
potential of

leadership potential
was exponential

according to most of
my raters

so heartbroken you
listened to my
haters

in case I lost you it's
the Army
personified

she was one of my
greatest lovers
longer than I loved
another so when
she asked me to
retrieve my keys my
belongings and
leave

maybe I was peeved

but it was hard to
breathe

I got to talk about
2010 and 2011

before I made my E-
7

I was in Atlanta in
heaven actually,
everything else was
dark as hell

job hell

you were the only
bright spot in my life

so I made you my
wife

took your son as my
own

so on that dark
dreary day why'd
you leave me alone

packed your stuff
and left

I checked and
checked

looked for a note
amongst the empty
hangers

empty drawers I
opened them

Did you know my
mind would swim?

strength would
leave again I
couldn't breathe

my faculties went
limp

I made a valid
attempt

I had to sound so
strong making that
phone call all I
wanted to do was
bawl, fall, crawl

but there wasn't
anyone else to make
the call

I told my boss who
was younger than
me that you left

without a note on
the shelf

yes I checked

I had to sound
strong like yeah I
got this

I'm just pissed

I don't even
remember crying

or untying my boots

it was so quiet

I couldn't buy a
sound

nor could I believe it

you gave me your
reason

keep it

these are some of
my darkest days

that blocked the
rays of sunshine in
my life

left by a wife my
other love politely
asked me to leave
with a hard shove

and then there's you

you hurt me deeper
than you'll ever
know

It's three-fold

I'M STILL STUCK

earlier today I got an image

it wasn't a gimmick

I was sitting in a crib

can't remember if I was in a bed

can't remember what I was wearing

but this is what I am swearing

you would leave us in the crib for hours

because you had the power

to change our diapers when they soured

we'd cry for days

others would be amazed

at how you were never fazed

maybe you were dazed

you wouldn't come to our beck or call

even though we were small

hadn't learned to crawl or fetch a ball

but we knew how to bawl

hoping you would come console

or give us a hug or hold

but you stayed on cold;

cold as ice not nice failed to suffice

chose not to splice

my future would pay the price

and the worst thing is

I'm still in this crib

RAZOR BUMPS

Often I wondered how did I learn to shave

when did I start to behave

as a man out of the fire into the pan

I wondered what was my daddy's plan

I mean did he think I could

or did he think I can

live without him and become a man

I am saddened by his absence

he's lived his life at my expense

he left and never made it make sense

I wish he would have stayed around

maybe if he had I wouldn't have almost
drowned

maybe it wouldn't have taken me so long

to be found

maybe he would have saved me

even if life wasn't gravy

it would have been nice

he was happy

he made me

he left without leaving a note

didn't even make sure I had a coat

or a boat that floats

no lifeguard on deck

my life was like a bad car wreck

you see the EMTs and hear the sirens

but you can't stop staring

music is loud notes are blaring

maybe I'm a little angry

still a little cranky

I mean I'm strong

but I don't think I'm wrong

I'm in a situation

and it's hard but I'm not escaping

so pardon if I find it hard to understand

why you didn't make it a priority

to raise your little man

VICKSBURG

Known for a significant battle in the civil war

and where union soldiers won a decisive
victory

I was ordered to attend a hearing

although I had 17 plus years

someone thought it necessary

my career end nearing

it was a long run, it was tough it was fun

but my loud personality

and telling others what I'm not going to do

can't be undone

I squared my hunched shoulders

all I can remember is being a soldier

I've been here for years

through blood sweat and tears

I've lost comrades,I've lost friends

saw careers end

some were fair some were grave injustice

unrighteously dismissed

under the guise of

the Quality Management Program

a complete sham

robbing well-deserving soldiers of retirement

well I must digress

back to the Vicksburg mess

I didn't deserve to be here

it wasn't about me failing to adhere

in order to be crystal clear

this was an attack launched in hate

well isn't this great

my fate in limbo based on hate

I can be obstinate

strong-willed hell I could be determined

give me a pulpit for my sermon

I need this to make sense

to uncover the resent

resentment hurt feelings disillusionment

brokenness depression

stifled refused expression

they were determined to teach me a lesson

they had all the power

and they were in the right cause

our relationship had soured

like expired milk

they were inclined to determine my guilt

had to hide my wilt

I was broken heart-mind almost the will

Maya Angelou, still I climbed

still, I rhymed

with reason

a tough season

but had to overcompensate

to hide the limp in my gait

so I made the most noise

he's still boisterous

passionate and explosive

I did the most because

I couldn't face my life

first the wife now this

how much more could I take

man I could be fake

I was strong; I pretended to be

couldn't let anyone see the depression

alcohol was used as a weapon

I killed myself daily

every burden they gave me

blackouts

pass outs

knockouts

I drove

you know how it goes

bars I've closed

I closed them every night

this was how I chose to fight

I didn't care if it was right

had to be up in the morning

bright-eyed happy and bushy-tailed

I couldn't face the fact that maybe I failed

failed myself failed the organization I loved

I felt shoved

unloved

I was all alone

I had to handle this on my own

cause it might not work out

couldn't focus on was it fair

my enemies would just gossip and stare

they longed to see me break

I have the backbone of a snake

my inner 8-year-old gave me this great
character trait

he was resilient resolved and resolute

stronger enough to refute

and able to stand in strong rebukes

so we stood there together

the good the bad the better

he's not fair weather

I started this poem thinking I was alone

but he was here with me all along

so I presented my case to the board

I let it all hang out

I left nothing to chance

a song and dance

a dog and pony

and the nomination for the Tony

did my best to not come across phony

they made the calls

they asked the questions

I called objections

relevance of the question

I'm offended at the suggestion

question lacks foundation

"Do you know what I'm facing?"

lacks personal knowledge simply speculation

leading the witness

back by popular opinion

"Retained!" "Did I hear you correctly?"

yeah they kept me, they saw through the lies

phony attempts and tries

fake alibis

I didn't commit S.H.A.R.P.

which was the spark

that made me aware of the dark

it was dark the whole time

I just paid it no mind, I'm legally blind

IT'S BEEN A LIFETIME

Fast forward rewind

I call on the hands of time

please let me take a second look

allow me to look into my life's book

yes even the parts I forsook

there are 38 long chapters

so for all the snackers and lip smackers

grab a snicker this is going to be a minute

I really wonder if it'll make a difference

or if it'll be different

I got to sift, shift, prepare the breach, and add

some adhesive to the rift

Heathcliff's and Clair Huxtable's

told me I was black beautiful and lovable

'Family Matters' tried to instill

family matters but my trauma spoke louder

than that chatter

nothings the matter not much laughter

my childhood

was some of my saddest chapters

my dad wasn't there

so, I grew up thinking he didn't care

I didn't consciously think much of him

that's what I think

I stood still along the brink

My life feels like one big kink

don't you dare think poor little tink

I grew up in a place that felt like the clink

we weren't freely able to pour our drinks or

grab cold tap water from the sink

we were banned to the dungeons

of our rooms

our rooms were cold

lonely and dark as tombs

where some of the sadness looms

I learned to groom I wasn't taught

my perpetrator was never caught

I'm supposed to love her and I believe I do

help me steep help me stew

for all she put me through

some would want me to focus

on the parts that weren't bad

but how do I when for so long I

disregarded that which made me sad

for all the good days I had

they were overtaken by the bad

iron clad shackled and locked away sometimes

we weren't allowed to enjoy

the brightness of day

hot as hell

not allowed to go outside and play

actually, it was either ordered or punishment

along the hours spent

in a dark unfinished basement

simply for being a young boy

or too much noise

of course, we fought

no place to release tension

or receive the desired attention

I was use to detention

I was beaten with an extension cord an iron

ore two by four and an iron cord

cry because my 8-year-old

wasn't allowed to cry

breathe sigh

he was too stubborn to cry

refused to break and refused to die

No, it wasn't sweet as pie

it took me 38 chapters to understand why my

little boy didn't die or couldn't cry

he was resilient and stubborn

he wouldn't give my mother

the satisfaction of being broken or torn

I'm just learning that it's because of him this

bright didn't go dim

I thought it was because of my strong

38-year-old self

but it's my little boy inside

I must thank for my health

I wouldn't have made it through tears and

years in my concept of strength

imagine the depth and length of his pain and

the courage to face the day again

he was rejected at birth

I'm convinced mother didn't want us

still, he rose refused to be stunted

through the pain, he grunted

he continued to believe one day he could
make

her happy though

she treated him crappy

he also believed she would

desire to make him happy

this is where loyalty

and hope are introduced

and 38 year old him is so confused

the wires are crossed

cause you must stay loyal at all cost

while hoping you change

I must be prepared

to be estranged

until your change

has been arranged

in actuality, I must first be loyal to me

even if it means being lonely

LIFE ANTAGONIZES

Miss-gives

straight up lies

it's commonplace

a cultural norm

who remembers the calm before the storm

matter of fact who cares

the warning sign

in the unbridled mind

no patience quick to resign

done it once or a thousand times

it's natural to be inclined to quit

when life begs for your grit

every bit of your energy takes away your
clemency

and makes you sit face to face with your
responsibility

the part you played in your demise

your lies

your gory story

with all the accurate details

your fails

your bondage and nights in hell

cold lonely nights imprisoned in your cell

you had the keys along somewhere

buried in your blue song

look inside oblige do the work

no clerk and no shirk

THE GREAT PRETENDER

I am not who I appear to be

for so long I was afraid to let others see

what if they didn't like the real me?

I've been rejected

this is how I have been affected

never been elected

never any real skin in the game

thought it was easy to be the same

but now I realize that was lame

I own most of the blame

others may think I am insane

so, I stay in my lane

never to share the thoughts in my brain

so, no more facades refuse to oblige

refuse to let you think it's okay to be you

while I am in prison

mentally not allowing others to see

the real me

no longer afraid if this makes me lonely

I choose to love me whether short or tall

big or small

in a relationship or by my lonesome

choosing to be wholesome

money stacks or money blown

sinfully or sin atoned

I'm worth being around especially if I'm
grounded

if you don't like that sound that is a problem
you have with yourself

being mindful of my health not just because of
wealth but owning the cards that I have been
dealt

no longer operating is stealth whether you
make a purchase or leave me on the shelf

I don't know if it was because I was ashamed
or thought it was better to be tamed if I was to
be blamed but I refuse to remain

getting off the chain health is the main
pretending is no longer something I'll entertain
even if you choose to abstain

THIS IS MY PAIN

I would love to
embrace

the positivity of
hope but at this
junction and scope

I'd rather embrace
the pain let me
explain and it may
sound insane

but I don't want to
be plain and though
it drove me insane

I haven't spent
enough time in it
and it made me
resilient as shit

it gave me grit

I can take life's
hardest hit

I won't bend or
break

my passion came
from the weight of
an insurmountable
tragedy and
sometimes it's
heavy

but if I'd rather sit
with the pain please
let me

I WANT TO BE A GREAT FATHER

Why bother

My dad didn't why
should I

am I better he didn't
leave a letter

didn't care if my
soul was in a fetter

didn't commit this
caper

but now I'll never
know why he left
and didn't tell me so

so I grew through
life with a pain as
sharp as a knife
wondering why I
was sad deep down
I guess I was mad

mad as hell didn't
know why so I
couldn't yell

too young to tell

couldn't speak
Braille

so get this

two parents one
present she should
leave

wasn't fast enough
to bob and weave
you left maybe
should've stayed

waters refuse to
assuage act my age
live within my wage
turn the page

learned these on my
own did you break
your phone cause
you never called
back

I think I was 12
that's probably
when I
contemplated killing
myself

Do you know what it's like when a kid puts the toy back on the shelf?

shipped returned to sender abandonment that sent me to a bender

it was time to render

time to engender

life hadn't been fooled

educated but time to get schooled

assets been pooled

war launched

stood staunch

played my role

the pain of you leaving took its toll

tried to roll

but had to admit the pain disdain

own it comb it

yes it hurt not a sweet dessert or a sweet dish nope not delish

but I'll be okay and so will my baby K

she is worth it and deserves my presence

a part of her true essence

a point of reference some of her identity

she got from me

I'll be here to answer her questions

I'll be by her side

regardless of where she resides

where she goes and	mine and her mom's
strides abides hides	relationship remains
she's my priority	a different story

ADMITTING PAIN

Now this is vital and this is a key

part of owning what was going on within me

I had to admit

relinquish my grit

although I'm tough as nails

can blaze a trail as hard as woodpecker lips

recovered well from most falls and slips

life was slipping through my grips

I had to bend if I wanted this pain to end

I had to bow, cry uncle and admit this pain

it served a purpose and it wasn't in vain

the pain teaches and reaches

cracks and crevices chinks on your armor

"Yes, You!"

I know you're a charmer

so was I

I'm glad my soul refused to die

it was hell I cannot lie

but it was worth it

I have to birth it

these skills I carry

limp wait or tarry

the pain...I had to marry

with my success

in the middle of my mess

while I navigated through my test

I learned, I leaned, I fought I even kicked

but I wasn't slick

I was chosen and picked

no games no gimmick

just admit it

then deal with it

DEAR SELF

Thank you for putting

your mental health first

from your date of birth

you've been on a journey

you're a major key a serious priority

you're amazing

a field for the grazing

you are a great guy

I'm glad you didn't die out there no lie

you're a forerunner

a trailblazer

a handsome heart breaker

I really believe you are going places

to see many new faces wealth potential

is exponential

I believe in you don't fret

for all you went through it made you

you are brilliant, resilient, intelligent, humble

you don't mumble

articulate

a great speaker

a truth seeker

you're genuine in tune

great with social cues

great points of view

one day you will fill pews

you'll get what's due, continue to be brave

your life it will save

you won't always be a slave

it won't be more potential in your grave

a great way ahead it will pave

give your past a wave

not necessarily the past the power

you won't always cower stand tall stand free

continue to own your story

soar to the top

don't look for the shoe to drop

you don't have to stop

the only person that can hinder you is you

there is no longer power and betrayal

you've learned how to wail

it's okay to fail and you have a ship to sail

most importantly;

your story to tell

THE KID IN THE CRIB

I promise not to trip

but I couldn't give it the slip

no one gave me a script tales from the crypt

about a kid in a crib

I refuse to ad lib not sure if I had on a bib

tears rolling down my face

grandma's smoke-filled up the place

standing next to my ace not sure my case

Kissa was crying up a storm

this was our norm

decided to write this poem

my childhood was insane

full of pain looking into this windowpane

me and my twin standing there crying

probably some whining maybe some pining

we wanted to be consoled

not to be trolled but our mother was cold

and now I'm too old to be consoled

but I am still looking for that ...

MOTHERS HOLD: PART TWO

So I'm here kind of nervous

kind of full of fear

I'm at my doctor's because she is my proctor

kind of like a spotter

I just gotta get to the bottom

find a place to slot 'em

dealing with the memories and feelings

because I have been wheeling and dealing

I've been smiling my whole life

but you can cut the tension with a knife

I haven't been me and maybe I'm guilty

so there is shame been living life maimed

had everyone gamed

because of the things I refused to name

it's not a blame game

it's the name my pain game

far from plain Jane

more than meets the eye

I have been living a lie hoping to slide by

and trying to be sly my, my,my,

so back to the doctor slash proctor

I'm removing my spleen

can't live in the in-between

finding out what my struggles mean

not a place for a teen

or to be sipping on lean

finally coming clean

looking into a mirror

my face is becoming clearer

I don't often like what I see

but here is a picture of a baby sitting in a crib

no ad lib my sister sounds like she's dying

I can feel her crying

she's screaming for this lady - I found out later

she made me, she made us

but she was acting suspicious

she let us fuss she was sitting on the sofa

and she refuses to come over

the image of me sitting

is not accurately fitting

that's adult me

how I learned to be

I'm crying too

come over mom and check on us

we are making such a fuss

she couldn't have loved us

is something I must face

I don't remember a sweet embrace

all my life has been a chase

needing her embraces

to remove the empty spaces

and that is something hard to face

even more difficult to replace

love should have been the case

don't leave us here for hours

wishing we had the power to change ourselves

to break the spell

that was my hell

and a place I no longer want to dwell

REPRESSION TWO

Memories trapped within the confines

of this brain drive me insane

a little disdain

difficult to explain

search deep within to understand

where I have been

did I sin how do I unlock them from within the
slide of this pen across the paper to commit
the greatest caper

nabbing memories of the night

attempting to conquer this plight

travel with all my might

illuminate the darkness with my light

turn the lumens up bright

to enhance my sight

I desire to get better to be a trendsetter not a
forgetter or a regretter

unloosed the tides that bind

open the eyes that are blind

gotta be patient and refuse to be anxious not
cantankerous

to clean up the dust to unearth them I must
the process I trust

it takes time to unwind to unbind

one day to intertwine

to conquer the thoughts and memories trapped
in my mind

I SAT WITH YOU TODAY

You took me on a journey

and reminded me of a place

you loved to play

you reminded me of so much

it felt as real as I could touch

you would roll those cars for hours

away from the area where you would cower

mom couldn't beat you there

as you played next to your uncle's chair

football played in the background

as you played at the bottom of the stairs

the place where you could just be

and display your full personality

where a good life remained a possibility

your first kiss happened in this very house

although she would never be your spouse

Justine lived close by

just a stroll down the street

Amber is there too your best friend

that you tried to make her sister your boo

she kissed you first

I remember Amber was mad as hell

but I was under her spell

her fond memories got me through

basic and AIT

we felt lucky

thank you for your time

for sitting with me

and reminding me about our history

the time you played with those cars

I promised we would never be far

and your voice

I won't bar or ban

from a boy to man

A LETTER TO MY INNER CHILD

Feel free to run wild

run wild my child

so many things I'd like to say

take a minute to play

pull up a seat and stay

no responsibilities, no bills to pay

imagine the childhood outside the fray without
the pain without the trauma

free to be

free to grow

free to do so

read a book

paint your dreams

enjoy your favorite ice-cream

get dirty

wear yourself out

be loud

not afraid to shout

dance under a water spout

no walking on eggshells

let your imagination swell

you can be anything you want to be

the canvas is blank

a teller at a bank

a soldier of war

own a grocery store

you can pastor a church

a chiropractor for the hurt

an astronaut on the moon

a weather caster covering a monsoon

a love doctor for lovers swoon

a chef in a restaurant

called the golden spoon

fly a jet, the sky is the limit

make sure your hearts in it

be a vet for the sick pet

climb a mountain

be an architect

an athlete soaked in sweat

ride a bike

lead hikers on a hike

fly a kite

lifeguard a beach

find a class to teach

be a farmer plant a peach

stretch yourself nothings too deep

keep sheep for little bo peep

underwater welder

build a house for shelter

you can be anything you want to be my

little inner child in me.

I MEDITATE

I sit in weight to investigate

the dire straight used to placate

subjugate just wait

play the tape confiscate

a lie in wait catch my breath

listen to it be mindful

present in moments own the moments

don't clone it or disown it

you didn't imagine it

it really happened buckled and fastened

choose a safe place and the right pace

rushing is a waste

a slow gait is better than to try to anticipate

which is another waste

fascinate a peaceful state

it's not a gallop or dollop

ADAPT

stew until it's done

victory is better when you've won

so are the prizes

the wake up when one realizes

the life track they are on

leads to the opposite of strong

It's not right or wrong

just depends on where you are going

you haven't been rowing

you've just been floating

your ego has been gloating

so we must abandon the inner IG

and refuse to ignore the inner kid

SELFISH

Pardon my new obsession

a release from the stressing on a new lesson
working on my progression

use to put everyone first

did myself worse

a low self-worth

celebrated my birth it's a new day

I have a new role to play starring role of me
my new responsibility hocus pocus

I'm now my new focus

I had to adjust quench my thirst

call me a lush I'm my own crush

so many years shed a lot of tears

kept a lot of fears scared to be alone

scared to go home scared to confront

scared to be blunt scared to be upfront

scared to challenge scared to save

scared not to obey answered every beck
answered every call now I'm about to brawl

a dilemma y'all I can't be afraid to fall, fall in
love with myself at least for my health my
mental agility to enhance my ability to center
my chi

putting myself first is key

mean no harm is the way it's got to be

things to achieve

I choose to believe in my importance

I'm significant

I'm taking my chance I will plant my feet

I choose not to fret rain snow or sleet can't
cheat everyone else must take a seat

I've got to accomplish this feat

not to be mean

I've got to be selfish

SUICIDE IS NO LONGER A VIABLE OPTION

My clinicians and doctors

would sure be proud

I'm no longer under this cloud

the days are still dark dogs still bark

but suicide has lost its place to park

it used to have menacing sharp teeth

silently whisper silently creep

we broke up we no longer speak

its voice was loud at its peak

March was dark darker because

I wouldn't face it

my hurt wouldn't let me embrace it

a strong stiff arm

a thunderous storm no alarm

no warning or waning

hesitating and fainting

it didn't let up

so dark and so stuck

yep it sucked

but I'd smile

all the while

crocodile tears formed

like cumulonimbus clouds

dark dreary gray

there had to be a better brighter way

without any other options I'd engage and let it
say what it would say

in church I'd pray

Father take my pain away

hell take me away

I no longer want to play

life beat me bloody

kept me feeling cruddy

the church was there

resentment formed cause

I don't think they cared

I love the Lord

but now it's a crisis cause

I can no longer afford

they should've had more options

more suggestions than cliché blessings

maybe there's anger

and fear of eternal danger

I don't point my finger

back to my poem and the fact

finally, out the black

and I'm gaining my life back

but I hope you can hear me

that I am articulating clearly

suicide has lost its teeth we broke up we no
longer speak

MY VOICE IS ENOUGH

My mom has passed and my dad is gone

neither asked if I was ready to let them go

they left without teaching me

what I needed to know

so, they been gone I'm still broken and torn

my heart aching and my knees are worn

I've been waiting for an eternity

for them to say well done my son

I have been yearning for their approval

the absence of their words

scream disapproval

this accusal does not activate the removal

of my life's pain that drives me insane

lock me away

because I use to say I'm okay

I have the unique ability to fight

another day

anticipatorily looking for

the ray of sunshine

that removes the binds and the confines

of the blinds over my mind's eye

so, I sigh in desperation perspiration

of the only possible explanation

the solution to the equation

of what I'm facing because I was tough

and my beginning was rough

it is time I realize my approvals enough

no further validation needed

the pain has succeeded

to illuminate what was needful

and though it wasn't gleeful

it made me as wise as a seagull who gathers in
groups stamps their feet imitating rain

main reason to call the earthworms

so they can eat them

Mom and Dad keep your words

I no longer need them

my voice is the seasoning

the reasoning and the dismissal

eviction ousting of reasonable doubt

for so long I've done without

and it has been hell

as the bell rings fighters in tandem

my voice has become my anthem

and three-point play and one

I'm just about done before your run

know that your voice is enough

that dispels your doubt

you no longer have to do without

affirmation no matter the situation

or what you're facing

take opposite opinions and erase them

whatever the flaws embrace them

end the marathon stop the chasing

believe your words are enough

and have the unique ability

to make the inadequacies meager

and insufficient ways of thinking run

and now I'm done

NOT JUST FOR THE BOOKS

Not just for the books

acknowledging the strength it took

to put this life on display

realizing I have something to say

so I choose gleefully this way

to jot my thoughts of the day

maybe to make it bright

for someone along the way

my mom refused to stay

she refused to love me

she chose to shrink my personality

refused to just let me be

now I make the choice to let others see

acknowledging others in the same struggle

use to juggle because my childhood

was smuggled

now I choose to tussle to lift up the rubble

it took life's trouble to un-humble

to take a second look on the double

looking introspectively

wondering if there was something wrong with me

now I choose to be free

no longer normally going against the grain

moving towards the pain

many would call me insane for inspecting life's
pain refusing to allow the disdain

to justify letting it remain

others would abstain

but I am retraining my brain

not giving my pain a lane or a pass

putting it on blast, strength to a mass

even if I have to be crass spend cash or lay in
the grass pain can kiss my ass

Epilogue

No matter the trauma you have faced, this is not your final chapter. I encourage you to get the help you need to heal from the pain. There is life after abuse, and you can have a loving family despite what has happened to you.

Break the chains.

Change the cycle.

Develop a life you were never granted for your family.

Ask for help. Lean on others. Access and follow a path that leads to success, safety, prosperity, joy, and happiness. The sky is the limit.

You survived for a reason.

Be the change that you so desperately desired to see for your future and the future of those around you.

There is hope after the pain!

The Facts

There are 4.1 million child maltreatment referral reports received yearly.

8.3% of victims are physically abused.

About four out of five abusers are the victims' parents.

A parent of the child victim was the perpetrator in 78.1% of substantiated cases of child maltreatment this year alone.

Resources
DYFS division youth and family service

https://americanspcc.org
https://www.nationalchildrensalliance.org

About the Author

Kerry Kinlaw was born in North Hampton County, VA and raised in Red Bank, NJ. After discovering he still harbored symptoms from the trauma of suffering 12 years of abuse as a child, Kerry decided to free himself from this pain forever.

Determined to kick the pain of the past *to the curb*, Kerry, a United States Army Veteran of more than 18 years, turned to writing poetry as a means to heal his suffering.

Kerry is a man who loves God and Jesus Christ with all his heart. A proud father, and sibling to four sisters and one brother, he is a gifted speaker and exhorter. Using his life's experiences to advise others, Kerry seeks to encourage others to face their truths and move forward past the hurts that may have been rendered unto them.

The author's intention for this book includes releasing the agony he suffered and inform others to never be ashamed of their pain.

"When I've served my time with the military," the author asserts with passion, "I plan to speak out against child abuse. I want to help others recover."

Thank you for your support

Made in the USA
Coppell, TX
11 August 2021

60306564R10081